Many Memories

Faye Yeaman Parnell Hooper

ISBN 978-1-64191-631-8 (paperback)
ISBN 978-1-64191-632-5 (digital)

Copyright © 2018 by Faye Yeaman Parnell Hooper

All rights reserved. No part of this publication may be reproduced, distributed, or transmitted in any form or by any means, including photocopying, recording, or other electronic or mechanical methods without the prior written permission of the publisher. For permission requests, solicit the publisher via the address below.

Christian Faith Publishing, Inc.
832 Park Avenue
Meadville, PA 16335
www.christianfaithpublishing.com

Printed in the United States of America

A Mother's Teaching

What have I taught you, child of mine?
Have I taught you first to love the true God divine?
Have I taught you concern for friend and foe?
For those whose character seems blighted and low?

Have I taught you God loves each one the same?
Be they heathen afar or a person of fame?
Have I taught you strength comes through each trial or test?
To welcome each day, try to make it your best.

That there is beauty in just simple things
One small blade of grass or a bird as it sings
That laughter with friends is a balm for the soul
To show loving respect for the young and the old.

That each day's new beginning gives one more chance
To search out opportunity in each circumstance.

Each sad experience has a lesson for all
If you are pure in heart, you need never fall,
If you have been wronged, to forgive and forget,
To not let little things keep you always upset.

To hold out your hand to another in need
No matter the color, the race, or the creed.
If you make mistakes, to admit it and then
Not to be foolish and make the same mistake again.

With God's help you can be triumphant over disappointment in life.
To be a peacemaker, not cause dissension and strife,
Not to brood over failures with regret and remorse
With faith you'll endure to the end of your course,
To glorify God in each task that you do
Help each person be better because of time spent with you.

There is dignity in hard, honest work,
From your share of responsibility, never to shirk
When you have convictions, stand for them bold
Live right day by day, make this part of your goal.

Have I taught you to cherish this land of your birth?
To honor and love it for all you are worth?
If I have taught you these things, I need feel no shame
For I know as a mother, I have not lived in vain.

Our Babies

You entered our world such a tiny mite.
To us, you were a lovely sight.
Those wee, wee hands, those dimpled knees
To look at you, sure did us please.
You filled our home with laughter that's gay,
Sometimes to music you would sway.
A king or queen, you seemed to be,
You meant the world to Dad and me.
You'd hug a kitten, chase a mouse,
Carry rocks into the house.
You grew so fast, time passes on.
You gave us gaiety and song.
We were held tightly in your grasp,
We cherish still your small handclasp.
The joy you brought to our small world,
Our baby boy, our baby girls.
Some memories fade so very fast,
The one of you will always last.
You'll always in our memories stay,
Our king, our queen of younger days.

This Family

There was Donna and Nancy
Joy, Steve, and Fred.
Sometimes you could yell
Till you almost lost your head.
They'd fight in the kitchen
Then run through the house,
Always hungry like pigs,
Or nibble like a mouse.
When at the table
Each in his place,
Our heads we would bow,
Take turns saying grace.
Sometimes meals were meager,
At times such a treat.
We never worried much,
We were thankful for something to eat.
Most times there was laughter,
At times tears were shed.
Punishment given,
One may be sent right straight to bed.
They are all grown and gone now
Each has a home of their own.
Some days seem quite lonely,
When you are left all alone.

Voices at Our House

"Who's in the bathroom?" "Me! I am on the pot."
"I'm gonna kick in the door." "You just better not."
"Can I have an apple?" "Will I get one too?"
"There's only one left." "Then an orange will do."
"You've got my pencil." "I don't see your name."
"That doesn't matter, it's mine just the same."
"Can I ride my bike up on top of the hill?"
"I'll come when you call, I promise I will."
"Can I have some new shoes?" "Well, I need some worse."
"We're too low on money." "Just stay out of my purse."
"The phone is ringing." "I am sure it's for me."
"Well, it's my turn to answer." "Oh, fiddledeedee!"
"Who had my comb? I left it right here."
"I didn't, Daddy." "Have you seen it, dear?"
"Gee whiz, I'm hungry." "You'll just have to wait."
"You'll ruin your supper by snacking this late."
On and on the sounds of these voices go.
Voices at our house that I love so.

A Great Guy

When I was just a little lad, I thought
I had the smartest dad.
He could fly a kite or throw a ball,
He was the wisest man of all.

Seemed he always took the time
To help me fix a toy.
My chest would swell right out with pride,
I was a lucky boy.

When there was something to be done,
He'd say, "Come on, let's do it, son."
We'd swim the lake or walk the field
To me, he was an ideal man.

Adolescence soon upon me.
I grew intelligent and wise.
Dad didn't seem to be the same.
Boy X was now his size.

His ideas seemed so ancient.
Expressions he used gets worn.
Could I have ever thought him
The wisest man ever born?

I knew it all, the world was mine.
How far my dad had got behind.
The gang I had, now they were great.

To be with them, I couldn't wait.
Boy, they were smart, they knew the most.
The things they did, how they would boast.

As I matured, things took a turn.
I found my dad was still quite smart.
At times I had almost broke his heart.
I long to be as wise as he, I'll do my best, I'll try.
Of all the men I have ever met, he's still the greatest guy.

Dad just sits back and seems to smile.
I guess he knew it all the while.

A Family All Grown Up

It seems the day will never come
When your family will be grown,
Then all at once they're up and gone
And you're left all alone.

The house that once seemed, oh, so small
The walls would almost break
Seems, oh, so huge and quiet now
Sometimes it's hard to take.

The laughter, sorrow, tears, and such
Seem, oh, so far away
You'd give just almost anything
To live again one day.

The noise that shook the windows
Or rocked the once-small house
Is gone and things are still now.
It's quiet as a mouse.

So when in lingering shadows
You sort of feel alone,
Just think of all the living
That made that house a home.

Almost a Man

You are almost a man, but still just our boy.
We're sad if you're sad, we share in your joy.
Seems you've been a boy for such a short while.
When God gave us you, he on us did smile.
The years in your boyhood are slipping away.
A man most a lifetime, a boy just a day.
God is always there, look to him in belief.
So forge straight ahead, look this world in the face.
You'll make a real man, you've got the stuff that it takes.
Success of a man isn't in his gold.
It's a life lived for God, not regrets when you're old.
Hold up your head, place it straight in the sun.
There is a job that needs doing, it's yours, get it done.
Almost a man, yet always our boy.
Thank God for a son that has brought us so much joy.

Our Garden of Little Girls Grown

Little girls grown, these three of ours.
They grew and developed like petals on flowers.

At times, oh, so happy, so carefree, so gay.
Sometimes pout or tease for most of the day.

They could work like a Trojan or skip to some song,
Then talk on the phone just ever so long.

They would hug you and squeeze you, say, "Gee, but you're great"
Then maybe the next moment, have eyes flash with hate.

School days soon over in the world with the throng.
You'd pray that your teaching would help them along.

They grew up so quick, time so fast seems to go.
There are some heartaches, for you do love them so.

As each walked the aisle, you'd think, "She can't be grown."
He would look into her eyes, place her hand in his own.

Now her love is for another, 'tis the way that God meant.
You know now your children were for a time to you sent.

Little girls grown, these three daughters fair.
Thank God for the flowers that grew in our garden rare.

My Dranma and My Dranpa

My Dranma and my Dranpa don't mind the jelly on my face.
Or if my hair is tousled and I jump around the place.
They seem to understand me more than any other folks.
They think my tricks are funny and laugh when I tell jokes.
You dotta have a Dranma who understands yer talk
And aint always yellin' at ya 'bout the way ya eat or walk.
Ya dot to have a Dranpa who thinks yer pretty swell
And tells the greatest stories that anyone could tell.
You really need a Dranma who thinks you'll turn out good
Even if ya never seem to do just what you should.
A Dranpa lets a feller feel just awful big and smart.
A Dranma gives ya hugs and says yer special in her heart.
Even if they scold ya, they don't make ya feel so bad.
Sometimes they say yer handsome and ya look just like yer dad.
I guess God gives us Dranpas to kind a fill a gap
'Cause you feel so safe and wanted when yer sittin' on his lap.
When I become a grown-up or Dranparent, old and gray.
I hope that I'll remember how it was back in my day.

Grandpa's Apple Tree

Our grandpa had an apple tree standing in his yard.
For our small legs to climb that tree sometimes seemed very hard.
We would look out o'er the housetops as we'd survey the land.
Talk about the things we'd do when we became a man.
We felt sure we were king of all the earth below.
When we would get in trouble, to that old tree we'd go.
We'd climb so high it seemed to us that soon we'd touch a cloud.
We'd sing and whistle way up there or maybe shout real loud.
The birds that nested in the limbs of that old apple tree.
We thought, sang songs much sweeter than any symphony.
The apples hiding beneath its leaves, no matter if sour or sweet.
When Grandpa said, "Just help yourself," we thought that quite a treat.
We may someday climb mountains high or become an astronaut.
Yet that old tree in Grandpa's yard will never be forgot.
In each child's life should be a tree in which to dream and play.
The time spent there stays in our memories as if it were yesterday.
There were other trees so straight and tall.
We loved that old apple tree best of all.
Just like our grandpa, so stanch and so strong.
A boy needs a tree that just to him can belong.
When that old tree dies, how sad we will be.
As boys, its gnarled branches held us quite tenderly.

Snowman! Snowman!

Snowman! Snowman! Where did you go?
Why did you melt away?
I worked so hard to make you.
Please come back and play.

Do you have friends in another land?
Maybe children over the sea?
I made you for my very own.
Come back and play with me.

I'll put a hat upon your head,
A carrot for a nose,
A woolen scarf upon your neck,
Two eyes of coal that glows.

It's lonesome here in this great big yard.
The earth is white with snow.
If you'll come back and play with me,
We'll have such fun, I know.

Snowman! Snowman! Where did you go?
Why did you melt away?
Don't you know I miss you so?
Please come back to play.

Doug's Monster

A brave boy of three, just a-creepin' down the stairs
Says, "Momma, I see a monster down there."
Quick, give me a gun, I'll shoot him dead,
Then I think I'd better sleep in your bed.

Paw, get me that pistol, there's a monster after me.
Then he dashed back up the stairs rather hurriedly.
Grabs Grandpa 'round the neck, tucks that little head out of sight.
Says, boy, that big monster, he sure is a fright.
He has one big eye in the middle of his head.
I'll shoot him first, then sleep in my mamma's bed.

Yes, a brave little boy, not very old,
Afraid of nothin', so we're told.
Down in the basement with his gun,
Lookin' for monsters, gonna shoot one.

An imagination as big as can be
Yellin', help me, Gradma, we'll shoot him, you and me.
Yes, I'm gonna shoot him square in the head.
Then I'm gonna sleep in my little momma's bed.

Carrie's Halloween

Witches, goblins, ghost, and such
Really scare me, oh, so much.
Chains that rattle when they walk
Scare me so I cannot talk.
They make me shiver to my shoes
With their oh's and ah's and ooh's.
They make me shake and quake and dream
Sometimes I wake at night and scream.
Reminds me of such scary things
Bats with big, black outstretched wings.
Sometimes at night when in my bed
I have to cover up my head.
I'd rather dream of things that're fun
Like dolls and bikes or bubble gum.
An ugly mask on someone's face
Just sends me home in a fast pace.
Big, black cats with fiery breath
Almost scares me half to death.
Halloween, you can call that fun
Just makes me want to scream and run.

Our Brenda

You have blessed each life that you have touched.
We love you, oh, so very much.
A pleasant smile on a radiant face,
Part of our Brenda's charm and grace.
Time spent with her is something you savor.
A grateful heart for each tiny favor.
We remember little things she said,
The darling way she tossed her head.
She'd treat each person, oh, so kind,
Tries to others faults, be blind
Her smile, the light within her eyes,
This little girl we idolize.
We wiped your nose when you would sneeze,
Bandaged up your skinned-up knees.
We bathed you, fed you, watched you grow.
Saw you excited, face all aglow.
To us, you are a precious girl.
You've meant so much to our small world.
Eighteen, now a lady fair.
You'll give your best no matter where.
This world would be a better place,
For those of every creed and race,
If each was half as sweet as you,
Our Brenda, dear, so true.

Grandma's Summer

My yard's a mess, I must confess, it's filled with children gay.
They kick up dirt, sometimes get hurt, they are busy all the day.
They laugh and fight, they scratch and bite, they are climbing in my
    trees.
They yell and scream, then in between someone gets skinned-up knees.
There're dirty hands, make-believe bands, some boxes torn to bits.
There are dolls and toys, there's girls and boys, at times they give me
    fits.
There are nails and screws, some words they use surprise you, what
    a shock.
There are hammers, wheels, some sneaky deals, someone may lose a
    sock.
There're cars and parts, there're boards and darts, there're drinks and
    ice cream bars.
At times I'd like to run away, or fly right off to Mars.
There're papers, sticks, and tastes and licks, there're gloves, there're
    balls and hats.
They break the rules, sneak Grandpa's tools, boy, they're in Dutch
    for that.
One may seem shy, how they can lie, they gather by the score.
If I dared, I'd hide inside and lock up all my doors.
They tackle me, they shackle me, I've sticky kisses got.
Yet even though I gripe a bit, I love each one a lot.
They're here, they're there, they're everywhere, sometimes there're
    nine or ten.
It seems to me they spend the day, just running out and in.
There're feet so bare, there's tangled hair, they beg for cookies sweet.
Oh, to relax for just one day, I'd call that quite a treat.

There're bikes and guns for everyone, or else there's trouble bad.
There are little kids whose mothers work and leave them with their
    dad.
If I get mad, I feel so bad to think I lost my cool.
I tell myself it won't be long, they'll soon go back to school.
They grow up fast, this won't all last, I'm waiting for the day.
Of leisure time I can call mine, just to dream the hours away.

The Questions Children Ask

"Can I please have a drink?" Where does water come from?
Why can't I have a cookie? Will you buy me a drum?

Where did my snowman go when he melted away?
Are witches real? Why can't I go out and play?

What makes a train stay on a track?
Why are some people white and some people black?

Can lightning strike me if I'm under my bed?
What makes Rudolph the reindeer's nose so red?

How come grandmas get so wrinkled and gray?
Why do I have to go to school every day?

How come you call the glass in the window a pane?
Can I stay outside and play in the rain?

What made you say that the ocean roars?
Why do I get so scared when my daddy snores?

How come mothers never go out to play?
Is that all babies do, eat and sleep all day?

Why is the color of some grass so green?
How come you make me wash so clean?

Can my friends come over and eat lunch with me?
How long is an hour? Can a blind man ever see?

Why can't I stay up and watch the late show?
Tell me, when it's summertime, does it ever snow?

Why do I have to do work every day?
While other kids never do nothing but play?

What will you bring me when you go to town?
How come they call a goose's feathers down?

Things Important to Me

My thoughts as I pondered and gazed up at the sky.
Was, What is really important to both you and I?
The budding of trees as each stands in its place,
To watch the leaves fall with such ease and grace.
The brown thicket pile, all covered with snow,
Where a family of rabbits run to and fro.
A chapel bell ringing out loud and clear.
Each time I hear it, it becomes more precious and dear.
My circle of friends, the pleasure they give,
Our freedom of speech in this land where we live.
A walk in the woods on a cool autumn day,
To watch squirrels gather nuts as they scamper and play.
The air that we breathe to be kept pure and free,
So very important to both you and me.
A leisurely jaunt on a quiet country road,
Hear the neigh of a horse, watch the hop of a toad.
See the sun shining through my windows and door,
As time passes, to me means more and more . . .
The friendly wave of someone passing by.
Isn't this important, to both you and I?
A Thanksgiving feast with our family and friends,
One of our traditions, I hope never ends.
Our nation's flag, waving for our country free,
Is worth more than all the worlds wealth to me.
The bountiful crops of grain and fresh food,
Some important things that make life seem good.
The honking of wild geese in flight to their feeding bed,
The changing of formation of clouds high overhead.

A young bride walking down a church aisle,
The face of the groom as their eyes meet in a smile.
The laughter of children so carefree at play,
Families gathered in church to worship and pray.
An aged husband's arm around his dear wife,
The one that he chooses as his partner through life.
The warm, firm clasp of a friendly hand,
To know wisdom is given by God to man.
Realize that love and respect for each person's life,
Could soon put an end to quarreling and strife.
That soldier boy's home from a land torn by war,
Would never need to return and fight any more.
On a cold winter day when life seems bleak and dire,
To feel the warmth of a friendly, cozy fire.
See growing plants pop their heads through the soil,
A father's return home from a day spent in toil.
The taste of water so clean, clear, and cool,
The character of those who teach our children in school.
A small chubby hand clutching a toy,
Sights such as these bring us moments of joy.
A Christmas tree lights a home full of love,
Grateful hearts for each other and our God up above.
Springs fragrant blossoms on bushes and trees,
What's more important than things such as these.
Sweet memories of loved ones so close to our heart,
The knowledge we'll be together, someday, never to part.
Appreciation for each blessing in this spacious earth,
Knowing God's in control of this vast universe.
Know the Bible is read in homes large and small,
Something so important to each one and all.
Again as I pondered and walked on my way,
My list was unending with new additions each day.

Harvesttime

What do I sow when I sow a seed,
Do I try to plant to meet another's need?
When someone is sad or seems quite forlorn,
Do I give them words so kind and so warm?

Have I carelessly watched someone's head held low,
Or have I tried to help their encouragement grow?
If I have been wrong or perhaps hurt a friend,
Do I try my best to make quick amends?

If I know a soul is weighted down with care,
Do I try to make things easier to bear?
Am I so indifferent to another's grief,
When time spent in prayer would help sustain their belief?

Do I forget my own shortcomings, not see my mistakes,
Yet think another's faults are, oh, quite great?
Have I, in some measure, sown discord or distrust,
Planted wrong desires, caused one small flame of lust?

Do I ever sow to the hurt of another,
When the message is clear to love each as a brother?
Will the seeds that I sow grow a field of wild weeds,
Or will I someday harvest a crop of good deeds?

Do I just go one mile when I should go three?
Do I try to live for my Lord constantly?
Am I really a blessing to others in need?
Just what am I sowing when I sow a seed?

When I'm in the judgment, will I stand straight and tall,
Or find fields I planted, grown withered and small?
Am I really the person I ought to be,
Do I glorify God, sow seeds of sweet harmony?

Soul Winning

Have you won a soul for Jesus?
Told a lost one of his love?
How he came from heaven,
Left his glorious home above?
Have you so soon forgotten
When you were lost in shame,
Someone gave to you this message,
"Trust him, believe on his name."
Tell them it is urgent,
That you must be born again.
That to God you don't belong,
Until you let Jesus take your sin.
Just tell them how he loves them,
Shed his blood upon a cross,
To redeem the souls of mankind
Without him all is lost.
Tell them he will save them
From a world of sin and strife.
The moment they accept him,
They receive eternal life.

Sunday School

Sunday school is a place where all people may go,
To learn of a Savior who loved us all so.
He died on the cross to pay for our sin,
All he asks of us, to accept and obey him.
While in Sunday school, pay attention and listen.
There isn't a word you will want to be missing.
So study your lesson to the very last letter,
This will please God and you'll learn to know him better.
So open and read your Bible, how grateful you'll be.
For the great love of God and for Sunday school free.

Procrastination

I said as I dressed to face the day,
I'll read some scripture then kneel to pray.
Before I had even washed my face,
Some other plan in my mind had found space.
Before I had hardly combed my hair,
I became too busy, no time to spare.

Indecision

You walk along a lonely shore,
The birds fly overhead.
You long to find yourself
Back on the city streets instead.

You walk the narrow sidewalks,
Rub elbows with the crowd,
Then wish yourself back on the shore,
The noise is much too loud.

Thankfulness

I'm thankful for the little stream that flows across a field
Thankful for the love we share that is so warm and real
Thankful for the sunlit skies, some clouds up overhead
Thankful for sweet memories or just a book I've read

I'm thankful for the tender look you send across the room
Sometimes it is the very thing to erase a moment's gloom
I'm thankful for the many times your hand may brush my cheek
Your firm, strong arms around me when I'm weak.

So thankful for our family, our friends, so dear and true
Thankful when each morning dawns that I am here with you
Thankful for this land of ours the home that we can share
For all the many little things you do to show you care

Thankful for the springtime, leaf turning gold and brown each fall
The things that I am thankful for, I could never list them all
I'm thankful for the gardens green or cattle grazing on a hill
The sound of soft, sweet music, ears to hear the whip-poor-will

Thankful for some busy days, the smile that lights your face
Thankful for our mutual faith in God's great love and grace
Thankful for a broad highway that winds around a hill
Or just a chance to sit and dream or walk around at will

Thankful for the men who love to till the warm brown earth
The laughter of grandchildren gay, to us how much they are worth
I'm thankful for the rainy days, the snow on bush and tree
But thankful most of all, dear one, that after all these years
You're still in love with me.

First Winter Here

We share the smell of a fireplace burning wood.
Look out the door, doesn't that smell good!
The snow is coming down so fast,
I wonder if this storm will last.
The tractor doesn't want to start,
We'll go to town and buy a part.
There goes a car, who can that be?
To see a friend is great to me.
I think the water's getting low.
Water truck can't get in this drive, you know.
The birds are hiding in their nest
As rabbits hop around with zest.
My goodness, but this snow is deep.
To live out here, we need a jeep.
I'll make some popcorn while we wait,
Or we can walk to Leonard's gate.
Too cold, we better stay inside.
What we need is a horse to ride.
Why don't we make a pot of stew?
Sounds good to me how about you?
I saw a fox out in the yard,
He's digging down and digging hard.
The days pass by, soon winter's gone,
We're ready for the summer long.

Remembering

I remember, I recall,
Days together, loved them all.
Early mornings' sunrise glow,
Sometimes playing in the snow.
Evenings spent in walks and such,
Always time for tender touch.
I remember, I recall,
Days together, loved them all.

If You Didn't Love Me

If you didn't love me,
I'd wonder why.
If you didn't love me,
I'd surely try,
To win your affection,
What it is worth,
If you didn't love me,
I'd feel accursed.
We've shared the good days,
We've shared the bad.
So happy sometimes,
At times, oh, so sad.
Living and loving,
These many years.
Laughter and joys,
Sometimes many tears,
Flowing so freely
From hearts aching and blue,
Again, I repeat,
For it surely is true,
If you didn't love me,
What would I do?
If you didn't love me
The way I love you.

A Long Time Ago

It was a long time ago, when our love was new.
A long time ago, you first said "I love you."
It was a long time ago when our dreams began,
It was a long time ago.

Our two hearts were entwined, the first moment we met.
Though a long time ago, I shall never forget.
We were happy, we two, with each other alone.
For us life was fun, just two kids not yet grown.

Just carefree and gay, so excited, we two.
I knew you loved me, you knew I loved you.
In three weeks we were wed, though poor we didn't care.
We had dreams, we had hopes with each other to share.

You so handsome and strong, we both so foolish and young.
You sang songs to me, then music rolled off your tongue.
In eighteen short months, our first baby came.
Then followed three more, life seemed such a sweet game.

Later we took another child into our home.
Loved him and raised him, he seemed like our own.
As our family grew, there were problems and trials.
They didn't last, they soon turned into smiles.
There were school days, vacations, picnics, and such.
All of this family loved each other so much.

Birthdays, graduations, soon wedding showers.
You were a king to this family of ours.
Soon grandchildren came, you would tousle their hair.
Tell them great stories, seemed you would always be there.

You wrestled them, chased them, scolded them good.
They just kept on loving you, they understood.
Then a few years ago, a shadow was cast,
Over our lives, that forever would last.
You became ill, our hearts all were broken.
We all shared the heartache with words left unspoken.

How I miss our days in the sunshine, our walks in the rain.
Though I am thankful, my darling, you now know no pain.
Still how I long to touch you, or just hear your voice.
I'll meet you in heaven, we both made that choice.
I do miss your kisses, the tilt of your head.
The way that you walked, how can you be dead?

I miss the look in your blue eyes, the smile upon your face.
Your hand squeezing my hand, your every embrace.
I am so grateful I had you, for those precious years.
There are times when I feel you are still very near.

You will be alive in my heart evermore,
I'll treasure each memory. You are my heart's door.
I cry for you, yearn for you, shed so many tears.
I shall always remember those wonderful years.
Was it really such a long, long time ago?

My Love

My love, two years have come and gone.
At times I feel I can't go on.
When in despair, I go to bed
Cradle the pillow that held your head.
The shadows deep the night so long,
Just once to feel your arms so strong.
I reach for you, you are not there,
You are in a land of beauty fair.
I cannot even touch your hand.
I'll meet you in the promised land.
We planned together to grow old.
Sometimes life is cruel and takes its toll.
Things are not as I wish they were.
Memories of you in my heart does stir.
Together we shed many tears,
Shared joys and hopes, sometimes our fears.
Our love was like a river that flows and has no end.
You were not only husband, you were my dearest friend.
Cherished memories of you I shall keep.
Forever in my heart buried so deep.

Spring Is Coming

Spring is coming. The birds will sing.
Reminds me of so many things.
Your old red cap. Your worn work gloves.
To see you do the things you loved.
To watch you walk your acreage small
Or try to give a wild bird call.
Sometimes a kite you'd try to fly.
We'd watch it soar so very high.
Feed the fish out in the pond
Sometimes let out a great big yawn.
Come in to rest awhile, some coffee drink
Then sit awhile to dream and think.
To plan the next project, you'd do
Or scrape the mud from your old shoe.
I miss the sharing of those days.
I miss you, oh, so many ways.

Memory Lane

I walked down memory lane today,
I knew I'd find you there.
It seems the only place I live,
Where you and I can share.

You held my hand, it was then I cried,
I just couldn't hold back the tears
For thinking of the love we shared,
Those many, many years.

I saw your smile,
I saw your frown,
Upon your cheeks,
Tears trickled down.

My memory lane is filled with you,
Forevermore will be
No one on earth will ever know
How much you meant to me.

'Tis God alone who understands
The breaking of a heart.
Together we will be someday,
To never, ever part.

Missing You More

Why do I see you at every door?
Why do I miss you more and more?
When I smell the flowers, trees, and grass,
It seems to me, I feel you pass.
I think about you each step I take.
You are in my thoughts when I awake.
I can see you fixing watches each day.
If you hadn't loved me, what would I do?
If you hadn't loved me the way I loved you.
When I travel the highway and hear our song,
I feel your presence so very strong.
Without you, I am a stranger wherever I go.
When we were together, I never felt so.
I watch for your face in every crowd.
There are times I call your name out loud.
There are times I hear you call me too.
If I'd never known you, what would I do?
Our family misses you so very much.
Your laughter, your council, your loving touch.
If you could return for just one day,
There are so many things we'd like to say.
We would tell you we love you o'er and o'er.
Each day I miss you more and more.

Our Last September

Do you remember our last September?
Do you recall the shadows grim?
We knew our time together
Was coming to an end.

Do you remember our last September,
When evening shadows fall?
I still remember our last September,
Those days we cherished most of all.

You said, "I am failing," but kept prevailing,
You didn't want to go.
How could I lose you, the world abused you,
We loved each other so.

We held each other, there was no other,
Just us and God alone.
I still remember out last September,
Our time has come and gone.

I'm all alone now, on my own now,
And when evening shadows fall,
I still remember our last September,
That's when I seem to miss you most of all.

The memories of those days
Are mine and mine alone.
I just thank God that together,
We have seen our family grown.

The mental health counselor asked me to remember and write down about Don, things I remember that especially remain hard. Then go through a door and leave them when possible.

Remembering

Things I remember about my darling husband. How he loved our babies and helped care for them when he came home from work. Making the hydroplane in the basement with Steve. How willing he was to take Fred to raise. Teaching the kids to drive. Checking Donna's ring, when Tom gave it to her. The way he checked each item for weight and the best bargain. His willingness to return any item that wasn't right.

The way he would remind me of a special song that had special memories for us. The way he liked to come into the kitchen and taste what I was cooking. The way he sometimes enjoyed adding a touch of something to the product. The little surprises he would bring me. The patience he had with small children. His impatience with older children. How he liked his new clothes the kids would buy him. How he loved to have coffee at his mother's house. How proud he was with the birth of each of our new babies.

The patience he had when repairing an object.

Working on the car and whistling away. How he loved to go out and look at cars with sis and Paul. Flying the gas airplane out at Swope Park, with the kids, especially, Steve, Fred, and Pete. The kick he got out of kidding Edna or Catherine about the sheriff getting them.

I loved to watch him play the violin. Watch his hands, how he held his tweezers when repairing watches.

He was so intent on his work but always had time to fasten my necklace or take a splinter out of my finger. That certain look he gave me when I would walk into his shop.

He would say, "Now, little lady, what can I do for you?" while holding my hand.

How if he left for work a bit upset about something, he would call back home and tell me he was sorry and tell me he loved me. Taking me for evening drives so we could talk without any interference. The large platter of French toast he would make for the kids on Saturday mornings. How he loved to fry mush for the kids and was so proud of himself because his was better than when I fixed it. How he would sing the song about a girl named Faye, to me, a song he had made up himself. See him set on the porch and watch his ducks on the pond. Him on his little tractor with cart he made, going over to chat with Harry. Him walking down to the burner with the trash to burn. Making popcorn, especially cheese popcorn.

The tears he shed when he said, "Please don't leave me in the hospital, as I'll never come out alive." Him thinking he had Parkinson's, when he was told he had Hodgkin's. The time they took a liver biopsy and had to wait to operate because his pressure went so low they almost lost him. How miserable and upset he would be when he had a flashback of his experience at the hospital with staph infection.

How he would ask me to sit beside him when he was reading the paper. Sitting in church with his arm around my shoulder. Looking forward to the cherry pie Mom made for him when we were going to see her. The phone calls he always made to me when I had to go alone to Mom's and he wasn't able. Teaching the kids to drive the boat. Teaching them to ski.

How when he wasn't able to do much and I did the mowing, he would sit on the porch and wave to me. Then at 3:00 p.m. always have me stop when he had tea and cookies ready for us. How hurt he was and how depressed it made him feel when they said he couldn't pass his last driver's test. How happy it made him when I talked to Dr. Bass and he said "Yes, he should be able to drive." How he enjoyed doing things with his family. How he enjoyed the IDs. How he liked to make chili.

How good he was to me when I did not feel well. How well he would clean up the kitchen when I was sick or real tired. How upset he would get with me when I would not buy myself new clothes. How he would grab me and dance me around the room at times.

How when Joy and Doug lived with us, he would romp and wrestle with Doug each evening. The time he had me call "Guys" when it was "Kitty Clover" chips that were stale. How well he enjoyed going to see the kids after his doctor checkups. The times he would make plans to do something with friends then feel too bad to do it after being sick. The fun he had calling Leonard, his foreman, when building the house. Each time he had a good report, he wanted us to do something special to celebrate after he had taken a treatment, like eating out.

How he acted the day Joy and I caught him at Taco Bell's. The look on his face when he asked me if I thought he was a good father. Him hanging diapers when he didn't work on Saturday. How upset he would get with the kids when we came home from the store and they would jump up in chairs to look in the grocery sacks. He'd tell them, "Just wait now." How upset he would get when it was time to paint the house. The time he bought me skates. The time he bought me a coffee table because he couldn't afford a dining room set. Little surprises he was always bringing. How he cleaned the oven for me because I hated that job. How aggravated he got with Warren because he raised a better garden. How he always planted salvia and marigolds. How he hated it because he couldn't provide more for his family. So many times when he would say how glad he was when the Christmas rush was over at the store. How he liked to make fudge. How he took over the job of making the fruit salad for Thanksgiving.

After entering the hospital each time, he would be at the door waiting for me to get there by 6:30 a.m. How he liked for the family to come when he was hospitalized. How when Susan was at St. Luke's, he looked forward to her visits. When able to do so, how he liked to go back to the lake. Wanting me to get in the habit of keeping my doors locked so when alone, I would remember. The horrible feeling I had the night he said "I feel like my body is turning to stone." The concern he felt about me having a home of my own, when he was gone, was just almost overwhelming. How it bothered him to think some misunderstanding might happen in his family. So many more personal memories that are mine alone, how he liked to rake leaves and to play in them with his grandchildren.

What good care he tried to take of his teeth and hated it because they had spaces between them. How he loved to hear the kids play their instrument. How upset it made him if he thought they weren't practicing as much as they should.

The time he sold Donna's accordion because she wouldn't practice.

The time he sneaked away to smoke after he stopped. Then felt so guilty he had to confess it. I was so thankful he was not a sports nut; even though he loved exercise and games, he never spent his Sunday afternoons watching games. "We needed that time together," he said. The Sunday afternoon rides we took with Harry and Vi after church.

The times he told the kids "No more pets," then changed his mind and ended up feeding their pets part of the time.

How he loved for us to take walks together in the evening after we moved here. How pleased he was when he saw me walking up the road to meet him, while he was still going back and forth to work, from here in the country.

How happy it made him after a blood transfusion for his count to go up. The confidence he had that I could make just about everything okay. How good he was to my dad and brothers. He loved to do things for Mom. He never seemed to hold a grudge. Was very protective of me if he thought someone was not doing me just right. Felt so bad when I had to do some things he felt was his responsibility. Was very concerned I would be left destitute because of his sickness. The times he begged me to sneak him out of the hospital in Camdenton and take him back to the lake, then home.

When Donna wore his shirt and he went in and put on her good blouse. How bad he would feel when he got upset with some of our family because he had said something ugly to one of them. How he always made me feel very special. How he always wanted to read a new poem I would write. If the sons-in-law did not treat his girls right, he just thought they should come home. But then he thought his sons-in-law were pretty special. How when he came home from work, he nearly always had something interesting to tell me that had happened that day.

How concerned he was about anyone else who was ill, but how he hated to go visit anyone in a hospital. How clean he was about his person; even when very sick, he still wanted to take his bath and wash his hair. The day he passed away, he insisted on a bath and washing his head before Joy came for us to take him to St. Luke's Hospital. How could I ever write all the things I carry in my memories!

My Legacy to My Loved Ones

What would I leave when my life is through?
A relationship sweet between God and you.

A desire to serve your fellow man
To help each person be the best he can

No houses large, no pot of gold,
Compassion deep within your soul

A zeal to understand God's Word
Help spread its message to be heard

No houses large, no pot of gold
Compassion deep within your soul

To keep your mind on things that are pure
The greatness of God and things that shall

Willing hands your work to do
To rest in peace when your day is through

Truthful lips and courage for right to stand
The privilege to live in this wonderful land

Your name written down in the Lamb's Book of Life
A forgiving heart toward those who sow strife

A continual yielding to the Holy Ghost
A life controlled by this Heavenly Host

No glistening diamonds, no stocks and bond
A conscience clear when each morning dawns

Material wealth, I'd not leave for you
But God's spiritual blessings all your lifetime through.

My Daddy

A-spittin' and a-chewin' and a-cussin' too
These are the things I've seen my daddy do.
Makin' a mistake and a-sayin' that he did
Sayin' no use to try to hide them, 'cause they can't be hid
Talkin' with his neighbor across the fence
Then swearing that his neighbor ain't got a lick of sense.
Hammerin' and buildin', maybe laughin' loud
Never wantin' to mix in with the city crowd
Down by the pigpen past the barn,
Him and another spinnin' some big yarn
Hitchin' up a team and a haulin' hay,
Working like crazy till the end of day
Out in the cow barn early in the morn
Milkin' or waitin' for a new calf to be born
Following a plow down the straight corn row
Or maybe in the garden weedin' with a hoe
Never givin' up though the task was hard
Helpin' butcher hogs and a renderin' lard
Walkin' down the lane singin' as he went
I can never picture him as old and bent
Chips a-flying as he chopped the wood
Trying to teach us to be kind and good
Sometimes scoldin' us yet lovin' everyone,
Takin' time for a little bit of family fun.
Now some rockin' in the evening by the firelight glow
Thinkin' of all the changes he's seen come and go.

Plain Folks

Fancy livin' is not for us
We share, don't crave no fuss and
I reckon for some, it's just fine
But we don't want it, me and mine
Feed us biscuits and gravy, beans
Not fancy livin' that turns folks' heads

A pot of stew with a slab of meat
Seem to us a real fine treat
Just a plain ole rocker, no contour chair
Keep your air-conditioning, give us
God's pure air.

We like livin' in spaces wide
Not crowded apartments and sittin' inside
We love the smell of clean clothes from a line
We're just plain folk, me and mine.

An old pump handle drawin' water cool
Let our kids walk not ride to school
A winding road with smell of clover sweet
Not a hot ole pavement that burns your feet

The hoot of an owl as he sits in a tree
That's the sound that's music to me.
The buzz of bees making honeycomb
We just ask for a simple home.

A vegetable garden, eggs gathered from a nest
These simple things we love 'em best
Where a boy finds time to lay in the grass
Watch the clouds overhead change shapes as they pass.

Livin' and learning from God's good earth
A chance to dream for all yer worth.
The smile from a neighbor goin' down the way
Maybe sit awhile to pass the time of day

See corn in a field sway in the breeze
Sights like these our eyes do please
High-hat parties and diamonds fine
Just ain't the thing for me and mine
A bellerin' calf by its mother's side
Makes our chest swell right out with pride

Just a walk down a lane and the smell of newly mown hay
That's really livin', we would say
Trade you places, not me and mine
We're just plain folk and like it fine.

Childhood Memories

A cellar door on which to slide
Sometimes skin off a bit of hide.
Uneven walls, some crooked doors,
No carpet covering on our floors.
Up in the hayloft we would climb,
Sometimes swing on a wild grapevine.
We'd pump the water, clear and cold.
"Don't waste the water," we were told.
Hear horses neigh and an old cow moo.
Each day discover something new.
A hidden nest, the violets bloom,
A childhood ended all too soon.
Shelves lined full with home canned foods,
Mittens, long underwear, flannel-lined hoods.
Hunt four leaf clovers in the grass.
A country school with few in class.
Run in deep ruts the wagon made,
Or sit and dream beneath the shade.
Hoe in the garden, on a washboard wash clothes.
Wear an old straw hat to protect your nose.
Help drive a team down a country lane.
Never know these memories could bring sweet pain.
Help dig a hole in which to place a post.
Biscuits for breakfast, much better than toast.
Oatmeal covered with cream, rich and cool.
Walk a mile or two to a one-room school.
A shortcut through a pasture around a pond.
Didn't need to worry about a neighbor's lawn.

Popcorn in the evening on an old wood stove,
Almost freeze your back and burn your toes.
Make snowshoes from a barrel slat.
Have such fun, just doing this or that
Heat a brick to warm your feet at night.
Snuggle down inside the featherbed tight.
Kick up clods as you'd cross a field.
Fish with a pole, no rod and reel.
Sit on the creek bed all the day,
Dangle your feet, plan your life away.
Carry wood, fill an old wood shed.
Help find a place for new pigs a bed.
Skate down the frozen creek a mile.
Not knowing would end in a short while.
Watch to see where a hen laid her eggs.
Hate the chiggers that would bite your legs.
The aroma of the orchard from the apple trees.
Smell of newly mown hay sometimes fills the breeze.
Plan all year for the county fair,
Families for miles around were always there.
Shadows on the wall from the old lamp light,
If the wind blew it out, you'd almost die from fright.
Very few toys with which to play,
Brothers and sisters more fun anyway.
Take your faithful ole dog and bring in the cows.
It seems things such as this don't take place now.
I feel sorry for folks whose memories
Consist of city streets and pavements hard.
Whose only playground was a fenced-in yard.
Who have never helped things of nature grow,
Like tomatoes or sweet corn in a garden row.
Never knew those memories of childhood sweet
Would help us as adults face the problems we'd meet.

.

Some of God's Gifts

God made the summer, spring, and fall
The changing of season, one and all.
Made the flowers in the springtime bloom
To help chase away the winter's gloom

The clean white snow and the thunder's roar
All these things and so many more.
The precious smile on a baby's face,
Nothing else can take its place

The birds that glide through the sunny sky
He made these all for you and I.
The fragrance of sweet blossoms rare
He placed them here for us to share

Made mountains tall and the valleys deep
The still of night for our rest and sleep.
The swaying branches in the forest green,
So many things to fulfill our dream.

The clouds that pass o'er the golden sun
The air we breathe free for everyone.
A silvery moon shining on a lake
While we so much just for granted take.

The strength of a father and a mother's love
Some of the gifts for our God above.
His most priceless gift was his only Son
Through him we find forgiveness
For the wrong we've done.

Two Worlds of Darkness

Oh, how sad to live in darkness, to never see a rose
Never see a baby's smile or a bunny's twitchy nose,
Never see a morning sunrise or a loved one's happy face,
Never view a glowing sunset or a turtle traveling a slow pace,
Never glimpse the rolling hills or the valleys down below,
Never see the splashing waves or a campfire's evening glow,
Never see the clouds that roll just before a heavy rain,
Never see the wind swept droplets beating against the window pane,
To never see a snowflake floating softly through the air
Or concern upon the face of a friend to show they care,
Never see the faltering steps of a person old and gray,
Never watch your children's games as they romp around at play.
Just to live a life in darkness, how depressing that could be,
Never see the leaves come falling down from tops of bush and tree,
To never see a bird gathering supplies to build a nest,
As it flits from limb to limb with such confidence and zest.
There is another world of darkness, that is by far a great deal worse,
To live in that world of darkness, you remain beneath the curse.
When you do not know the Savior as your very, very own,
Then you walk in spiritual darkness, you must walk that way alone.
Though you cannot see a sunset at the closing of the day,
You can see with eyes of spirit, God has planned a better way.
So accept God's grace and mercy, place faith in Christ the sacrifice.
You'll not grope in spiritual darkness, you will have a brand-new life.

Time

Now is the time to live as we should,
Now is the time for lives kind and good,
Now is the time to trust in the Lord,
Now is the time to feed on his Word,
Now is the time to stand for what's right
Now is the time to pray with our might,
Now is the time for salvation free,
Now is the only time there will be.
Now is the time for convictions strong,
Now is the time for our time isn't long.

My Desire

Lord, give me a glimpse of the bright morning sun
Contentment and peace when my day's work is done.
Thoughts that are pure, a mind stayed on thee,
Eyes searching for beauty in the things that I see.
A tongue so controlled by spirit of love,
The words that I speak inspired from above.
Goals high and lofty, others' hurts understood.
To know that your will is for my highest good.
Give me laughter and song that will glorify thee,
A desire to see others' happy and free.
Give me the strength that I need for each day,
A zeal to serve those who pass by my way.
Give me desires that are pleasing to you,
Abiding trust in you all my life through.

The Place Where I Worship

The place where I worship
Plain, I don't deny.
We meet there together,
My Savior and I.

It may be just a building,
Not at all up-to-date.
The story of love I hear there,
Oh, how great.

Our pews aren't padded.
We don't have a steeple.
My, what a pleasure
To be with God's people.

We don't need an organ,
Nor carpets so rare,
Just the joy of God's presence,
As we worship there.

The place where I worship
Can be anyplace.
For I am God's child,
One who's saved by his grace.

Eternity

I planted a seed, and it grew a tree,
A tree will not live for eternity.
I planted a seed, and the tree grew tall,
Cool shade for summer, firewood in the fall.
I planted a seed in the heart of a child,
So full of energy, so carefree and wild.
The child grew just as fast as my tree,
His soul shall live throughout eternity.
The fire in his heart, which way will it burn,
To serve himself or to God will it turn.
I planted a seed in a tired mother's breast,
She thought, for her family, she had done her best.
She thought, material things, so important were,
Found her spiritual influence had been mostly a blur.
I met a lady, old, bent, and gray,
Who felt her life had been wasted away.
When I told her about the grace of God,
She bowed her head and said with a sob,
"Why hasn't someone told me before,
If I'd only known, now my life is near o'er."
I talked to a man with a life all wrong,
Now he has turned to God, in his heart is a song.
In every life, there is such a great need.
Be very careful when you plant a seed.

What Are We Like

What are we like, we all want to know.
Like dark, threatening clouds, or a warm firelight glow
Like birds flying high in a sky azure blue
Like nights bleak and cold with no moon shining through
Like days on a desert so hot and so dry
Like toasting a cause with glasses raised high
Like sweet tender words from a loved one so dear
Like the fear in a heart when danger is near
Like a horse stretching its legs in a race
Like an atom crawling in infinite space
Like a great disappointment that leaves you depressed
Like the exhilaration of a howling success
Like a small frightened child afraid of the dark
Like a brave mountain climber out for a lark
Like blizzard winds across prairies bare
Like bees gathering nectar from plants here and there
Like a dream coming true when all hope is gone
Like stuck in reverse when you wish to go on
Like snowflakes so white as they softly float past
Like something to cling to, something to last
Like a queen or a king stately wearing a crown
Like sometimes so up, like sometimes so down
Like a swan gliding leisurely over a lake
Like the turbulent force of a spring earthquake
Like sunshine and flowers, rain from the clouds
Like walking on air yet fearful of crowds
Like snow-covered mountains or valleys so green
Like trees growing tall or stones in a stream

Like children with playmates so carefree and gay
Like hoping for rest at the end of the day
Like charging wild bulls or snails traveling slow
What are we like, does anyone know?
Like actors in plays or planes in the sky
Sometimes wanting to live, sometimes wishing to die
Like tigers or lions or scared little sheep
Like skiers who ski over snow white and deep
Like dancers onstage going round in a whirl
Like little boy blue or a tiny sweet baby girl
Like the mysteries of heaven to us here below
What are we like, does anyone know?

My Special Sister

If I picked a sister, she'd be just like you,
A smile warm as sunlight, a heart faithful and true,

The same sweet person if with pauper or kings,
One who finds joy and pleasure in life's most simple things,

One who could laugh at my silly ole jokes,
Show loving concern for less fortunate folks,

With deep understanding for someone in sorrow,
Who could help them have faith in a bright tomorrow,

One of life's richest blessings has been knowing you,
I think you're pretty special—sisters like you are few.

Through the Years with Your Sweet Susie

Susie, precious baby, oh, what she was worth,
A little gift from the heaven, sent right straight to earth.

Big brown eyes, fat dimpled knees
She'd hop and skip and others tease.

Her baby days were soon behind,
Somewhere in the past.
Yet memories that you cherish,
You know will always last.

Childhood games, Bluebird days,
Then came adolescence.
Campfire girls, oh, such fun,
Also piano lessons.

High school parties, picnics,
Movie dates and swimming,
There were times, when all alone,
Tears, your eyes were dimming.

Clubs and pep squad, football queen,
Engagement days, when young girls dream.
You love her so, this precious girl,
She kept your household in a whirl.

Wedding dress now in the making
Marriage vows, she'll soon be taking.
On Daddy's arm, now down the aisle,
You don't dare cry, you try to smile.

When she moves and takes her things,
To all of these memories, your heart clings.

Down through the years, you'll closer be,
She's still your precious girl, this Sweet Susie

Your Precious Son

A little boy with eyes so bright,
Brown tousled hair, sometimes he'd fight,
His teddy bear held by one ear,
To him it was so very dear,

A sloppy shirt or sweater torn,
A pair of shoes with soles well worn,
A cub scout suit, a ball, a bat,
Sometimes collecting this or that.

The peanut butter jar cleaned out,
Trombone and music strewn about,
A football hero, skinned-up knees,
You'd watch his games and almost freeze.

Now train and bike toys of the past,
He made his choice to fly planes at last.
Vacations, holidays, and family fun,
Some fond memories with your precious son.

Now your precious son is away from home,
No more a boy, now a man full grown.
You taught him faith and to honest be,
Fairness, squareness, and integrity,

That good, hard work would harm no one,
For the right to seek the evil to shun,
To forge straight ahead like the best of men,
When he makes mistakes to try again,

No shortcut to success on life's highway,
To keep pressing on, to take time to pray.
He has found the one who will be his wife,
Together they are planning their future life,

With mixed emotions, you'll see them wed.
As you think of their trials and pleasures ahead,
May God shower his blessings on the life of your son,
As he and Marsha are united as one.

A Parent's Prayer for a Son in Service

Dear God, he seems so young to cross our seas
Face hardships, danger, and disease.
They placed him in a special school
So he could fight in a war so cruel,
For other sons, we ask the same
You know them, Lord, each one by name.
Please, may he feel your presence there
When on the ground or in the air.
Should he be hurt or ill and frightened
We pray, you, God, his burden lighten.
He's young and brave, at times seems just a trifle bold.
Please keep your arms around him, Lord, he's not so very old.
He's just now turning twenty-one. Don't let him die in vain.
If it's your will to take him, Lord,
Please make it quick with little pain.
You didn't promise life of ease. Just strength for daily tasks.
To know your nearness whatever befalls, is all we ask.
Please stay beside him all the way.
Renew his courage day by day.
You gave your son. We may give ours, out in that war-torn land.
We ask no other favors, Lord, just keep him in your hand.
He left this land of freedom that others might be free.
We ask now that thy will be done, we commit his life to thee.

Ribbons for Valor and Medals of Gold

Ribbons for valor and medals of gold,
You can feel nothing, you are cold, you are cold.

A young man so brave, he flew many missions,
He gave his life, gave up dreams and ambitions.

You know not the cry of a grief-stricken heart,
You care not that a family has been torn apart.

Could you share in our joy at the time of his birth,
Share our feeling of sorrow as he was laid in the earth?

Did you feel the tug of that once-tiny hand,
His firm handclasp when he became a man?

When he left his homeland and family so dear,
Did you feel as he when asked to face that one dreadful year?

Can your medals of gold substitute for his life,
So soon snuffed out in a land filled with hatred and strife?

Can you comfort his mother, light up the eyes of his child,
Bring again to his father's face one happy smile?

Give strength to his wife at the close of the day,
Cuddle his tiny child and teach him to pray?

You are medals of honor with no living part,
Can you feel the ache in his sister's broken heart?

Have you kissed your son for one last goodbye?
Can you know what it means to have a husband die?

Can you wipe away just one loved one's tears?
Can you share in the memories of his former years?

Do you know of the longings through sleepless nights?
Did you shed your blood for another's right?

You cannot suffer our tragic loss for one moment of time.
You know not the meaning of words such as these: he was mine.

Can you feel our anguish, agony, or our despair?
Can you ever show someone that you really care?

Can you feel our sadness, the tears that are shed,
When the message arrives that a loved one is dead?

Can you ease the misery, the grief, or the pain?
Can you assure his loved ones they'll see him again?

You cannot fill the void of a broken heart's need,
Take the place of a son through given for his heroic deeds.

Do you understand when a circle is broken,
The message you bring with words left unspoken.

Can you place a wreath upon his deep grave?
You can never understand who it was that we gave.

Distinguished crosses and purple heart,
In some of our lives, you have become a part.

But God in his love understands, and he brings
The only message of hope, for you are not living things.

Ribbons for valor and medals of gold,
You can feel nothing, you are cold, you are cold!

Roses and Thorns

A rose and a thorn grow side by side
Beneath the beauty of the rose, the thorn may hide.

When rose petals fall away,
As the rain and sun take their toll each day

The thorn grows larger with no beauty there,
With the rose now dead, it seems ugly and bare.

The birth of a rosebud is a beautiful sight
All who look on it feel a glow of delight.

The thorn will always ugly remain,
But the beautiful rose will bloom again.

When the gardener prunes the stem of a rose,
The blossom sweet more beauty shows.

The thorn can never bloom at all,
Just prick and hurt when the rose petals fall.

Let's hide some thorns along life's way,
Help others not to the thorns fall prey.

Don't be a thorn where the blossoms die,
Let's spread more beauty, you and I.

For as the rose fragrance fills the air,
The thorn holds no beauty that it can share.

Sweet memories like a rose can make hearts glad,
It's memories filled with thorns that make hearts sad!

Poem for Thad

A letter to my little son I never saw:

Dear little son I never saw and though you never knew me,
I wish for you a life of pleasant times, not one that's sad or gloomy.
You'll miss your dad, I know you will.
Just remember that I love you still.
I wanted so to stay at home just be there for your birth.
When the message came to me, I thought I owned the earth.
A baby boy, my, I was glad.
What a wonderful privilege to be your dad.
I thought of trips someday we'd take, maybe fly real high.
You'd sit there in the seat by me, we'd glide around the sky.
We'd romp and play, have such fun. Buy you a pet, some fuzzy pup.
Your mom would probably say, "Won't you two ever grow up?"
We'd tuck you in your bed at night after we heard your prayers.
I'd be as proud as man can be, I'd really put on airs.
I wanted so to see you as a young man going to school
Getting lots of knowledge, son, yet sometimes life is cruel.
It wasn't meant to be my way. Our life we just can't plan.
You'll understand someday, I hope, when you become a man.
Don't let this make you bitter, son, we know God's way is best.
Sometimes our trials hard to face are really just a test
Look after Mom and be a son of whom she will be proud.
When on that day in heaven we meet, we'll sing and shout real loud.
God sent us you, we know that, son, though short together was our time.
I am thankful that I had you both, what joy that you were mine.
I never got to hold you close before my call to give.
My life's for God and country, so please, for God and country live.

Though I may never hold you or bounce you on my knee.
My little son, remember you meant the world to me.
Though in this earthly life of yours, I may not have a part.
You are held closer than you will ever know, for I've held you in my
   heart.

I love you, your dad.

My Bowl of Blue

A little mixing bowl of blue,
I use it, oh, so very much
I think of you each time I touch,
This bowl of blue.
It's really just a perfect size
For mixing dough when making pies
When moving to your nice new home
You left it sitting on the floor.
You didn't need it anymore.
Said, "I should take it home with me"
It seems I use it regularly.
I've mixed up noodles for some broth,
Slopped food upon my tablecloth.
I've used it making cookies too.
I'm glad that with it you were through.
It's held so many birthday cakes,
That ended up in stomachs.
For making salads sweet or tart,
In every meal it's had a part.
It's held chopped nuts and apples too
This little mixing bowl of blue.
It doesn't match a thing I own,
But has a place within my home.
If it gets broke, what will I do?
I love this little bowl of blue.

The School of Life

You spend years inquiring and searching,
Figuring out problems, both great and small,
No matter how wise or the method,
You never will answer them all.

You long to acquire so much knowledge,
Each day how much smarter you'd grow,
But the things not in books yet important,
We learn in life's school, this you know.

Some men gather wealth and build castles,
Never finding contentment and peace,
While some men, though poor by world's standards,
Have found riches that never will cease.

Each pathway you take's an adventure,
No matter how fast or how slow,
The thing most important is learning
That God's way is the wise way to go.

We are proud of the things you've accomplished,
Though your goals keep you near or afar,
If you're happy, you're successful in our eyes,
We are proud of the man that you are.

We all love you and want you to know it,
We're behind you each step of the way,
May your pathway be bright as the sunlight,
As you travel through life day by day.

A Friend

The love of a friend is a beautiful thing
It can make the heart glad, make you just want to sing.

At times if you're lonely or feeling quite blue,
Just a word from a friend can mean so much to you.

Life is really worthwhile when a friend tried and true,
Can share in your sorrow or laugh with you too.

A world without friends would seem worthless and bare
'Tis the love of a friend that helps your burdens to bear.

The love of true friends is a joy to behold
Something I wouldn't trade for the world and its gold.

Friends

True friends are hard to find. They are of untold value.

They are someone who loves you even when they do not understand you.

They want the very best of all good things for you.

They try very hard to accept you just as you are.

They are your ally. They are one of God's priceless gifts to you.

I can say to you, "Thank you for being my friend."

Friendship

Yes, the world is wide and the world is hard
There is little or nothing new.
But the sweetest thing is the grip of the hand
Of a friend that is tried and true.

Your Rose Marie

I saw her walking down the aisle
In veil and gown of white
She looked just like an angel
A very lovely sight

I saw him place a tiny ring
Upon her hand so fair
I saw them at the altar kneel
And ask God's blessing there

There was no doubt within my heart
That this was meant to be
This precious girl I am speaking of
Yes, was your Rose Marie

I, for a moment, closed my eyes
And turned back several years
Was awfully hard for you, no doubt
To hold back many tears

For God had placed beneath your heart
A tiny mite so wee
And when she came into this world
You named her Rose Marie

I saw you hold her in your arms
A chubby lass of three
With winning smile entwining hearts
This very Rose Marie

I saw her with a mamma doll
Held in her arms so tight
I saw her skipping off to school
Her eyes so shiny, so bright

I saw her as she took a fall
Bring you a skinned-up knee
You doctor it and wrap it up
Then kiss your Rose Marie

I saw her in her high school days
At parties, oh, such fun
It's very hard to realize
She's grown, this little one

You haven't lost her, I am sure
That you will closer be
Because you've been a mother grand
To your girl Rose Marie

That Special One

You've picked the one to share your life!
You'll be to him a precious wife!
You'll walk together hand in hand!
May spend some time in a foreign land.
Sometimes you'll feel depressed and blue
Away from friends and families true,
So just look up and know God's there
He will help you each of your problems bear.
As you learn to cook, wash, mend, and clean,
Just laugh and on each other lean.
You'll learn to budget every cent,
Know where each dollar went you spent.
Will be such fun to plan your home,
With someday children of your own.
This new life will be lots of fun,
Now that you've found that "special one."
Life's richest blessings and lots of luck,
To a wonderful couple, you and Chuck.

Your Linda

She's grown, your precious daughter
It's so hard to believe
The time is almost here now
Soon from your care she will leave

She came this darling baby
In fulfillment of your love
You felt sure God in heaven
Had sent her from above

This tiny tot with smile so rare
You hoped would never know a care
This little girl with hair so gold
Your happiness in her hand could hold

At times so thoughtful, sometimes quiet
At times just filled with sheer delight
She'd pet a puppy or climb a tree
Just run and jump with childish glee

You loved to hear her laughter gay
Or see her to some music sway
A princess fair, she grew to be
She filled your life so perfectly

Some happy days, some sad days
Some memories yours alone
The times that you will cherish
These years seem to have flown

Don't ever feel you've lost her
Just because she's grown
You've been the grandest parents
Any child has ever known.

Mary Ann

This little girl with face aglow
This little girl you didn't know
Found her way into your heart
Of your life, became a part
You prayed so for a baby
Then Lord sent some small child
You didn't know Mary was for you all the while.

She'd toss her head and roll her eyes
You thrilled to watch her grow in size
Her tiny hand would hold yours tight
Oh, what a thrill of sheer delight
Hopping, skipping, jumping all about your home
To think that it was true, she was your very own.

With little head on Daddy's chest
A lump of pride would fill your breast
When she was sick, with tender care
Your loving arms, she knew was there
Roller-skating or on her bike
She filled your life, this precious tyke
Grade school, high school, graduation
You felt proud, complete elation.

Her baby blanket, you did keep
Those tiny things that makes one weep
Some priceless memories, things quite worn
You felt to you, she had been born

Two tiny tots have won your heart
Now of your life, they are a part
They wrap their arms around you
Those chubby sweet wee hands
Belong to the children of your own
Mary Ann.

Our First Daughter

We've longed so for a daughter,
Jeanette, you'll be the one,
We'll love you like you are our own
Because you love our son,

We'll try so hard to please you
We hope you'll love us too,
For if you make John happy,
That's all we'll ask of you.

We'll help you if you need us,
Try hard not to interfere
A daughter-in-law is not close enough
To us, you'll be too dear

We feel that God has blessed us
By bringing you our way,
Because we'll have a daughter
On our son's wedding day.

Your Karen

You're going to see your Karen,
Who feels so wise and grown,
Decide to leave your loving care,
Start a home that's all her own.

Though grown, it isn't easy,
To see one walk the aisle,
You'll shed some tears,
No matter how hard you try to smile.

So as the tears caress your face,
Let happy memories take their place,
Remember when a little girl,
She seemed to keep things quite a whirl,
Her laughter gay, her twinkling eyes,
Sometimes her words, one big surprise.

Like little birds, our children
Must someday leave the nest
Then start a home that's theirs alone
With one they love the best.

If sometimes you feel lonely, and her very much,
Just be ever so thankful, someone enough
To work for her and love her, try her dreams come true,
You know, you really haven't lost, she's gained a son for you.

Heaven on Earth

A radiant bride,
A happy groom,
A small apartment
Not much room.

It seems so like a castle
When two are so in love
You feel so strong the blessing
Of God straight from above

Bright gifts and ribbons strewn about
Thank-you card, fun to send out,
Those happy days that two can share,
There's nothing else can quite compare

There will be misunderstandings,
Times all won't seem so gay,
Yet you can work each problem out
Your love will find the way.

So through your years together,
Just put each other first
Then you'll have learned the secret
Of heaven here on earth.

The Beginning of Wisdom

I can't claim much education, I just ain't as wise as some,
Yet when it comes to common sense, I ain't exactly dumb.
I know that all our sinnin', it ain't pleasin' to the Lord
He tells us love each other, it says that in his word.
His Word, the Bible, tells us, to another be ye kind,
Even with our heap of schoolin', we travel far and wide.
My, don't we think we're something, 'cause he made that same mistake.
We just better pay attention about that fire and brimstone lake.
Materially, I sure ain't rich. I don't know about punctuation.
I know it's only by God's grace we've been blessed in this nation.
You can call yourself a wise man, have diplomas line your wall,
If you ain't learned Proverbs 1 verse 7, you just ain't smart at all.
You may have gone through college, spoke before some crowds so
      great.
Think my beliefs quite old-fashioned, just not one bit up-to-date.
If you really long for wisdom, search the scriptures, better start,
I just wouldn't trade you places. I've got peace down in my heart.

True Judgment

You can't judge another by the cut of his hair,
The shape of his face, or the clothes he may wear,
The amount of his wages, big diamond rings,
God alone is the judge, another by the make of his car,
If he has stayed close to home or has traveled afar,
By the size of his house, mansion or cottage small,
For God is to be the final judge of us all.
You can't judge another if he's lonely or sad.
God alone knows his heart if its good or it's bad.
You can't judge another by this wicked world's views,
Or because he's quite prominent or has made headline news.
You can't judge another because of his race.
The one righteous judge, we'll each meet face-to-face.
You just can't judge another by the way that he looks
Or the time that he spends to get knowledge from books.
You can't judge another by his actions so kind.
You don't know the thoughts that at times fill his mind.
You can't judge the one with a smile on his face.
He may have no concern for God's mercy and grace.
You can't judge another when he's laid beneath the sod.
Be thankful, my friend, that the true judge is God.
We each can be wrong in the things we can see.
I'll try not to judge you, please try not to judge me.
So don't worry about mankind, what he may think of you.
Just strive to please God for his judgment is true.

The Tail Dragger

Lady Sadie and the Prince of Wales paraded the yard with their high-held tails.

Poor ole Arby, he could not go, 'cause his old tail just dragged too low.

He would whine and he cried 'cause the grass was deep.

So he stayed on the porch till he fell asleep.

He felt like he was just left out.

What in the world was that all about?

He would check the tires if a car came in.

He knew that brought a hug for him.

So let Lady Sadie and the Prince of Wales just show of their ole high-held tails.

My Treasures, My Children

You are a treasure to have and to hold
Worth more to me than all the world's gold
The chest for my treasures is hidden in my heart
I am thankful in your life, God gave me a part
A gift from the Heavenly Father above
He laid you in my arms to share you his love
You are a treasure, a treasure to me
A treasure more precious than any could be
If I climbed the mountains or searched the sea deep
I could not find a treasure so joyous to keep
A crown filled with jewels would mean much to some
You are my jewels and my crown, I love you each one
A treasure of value more precious than lands
A treasure to hold in my heart and my hands
You are a treasure, a treasure to me
A treasure more precious than any could be
My Donna, Nancy, Fred, Joy, and Steve
You are a treasure, a treasure to me

Mom, 2004

Tinker Speaks

I jump and romp around with glee
If you take time to come pat me
I'm hoping that you'll understand
I love you when I lick your hand
I look at you with eyes so sad
Especially if you call me bad
I'll always to you faithful be
Oh, please take time to walk with me
It seems no matter what you do
I never hold a grudge toward you
I am aware when you feel grief
I bark to keep away a thief
I've loved you since I was a pup
I wish you wouldn't tie me up
"He's just a dog," I hear you say
But like a child, I love to play
Even though I like to roam
You know I will always come back home
I am your best friend, the experts say
Please keep me. Don't give me away

My Tribute to You, Bill

You came to me when my days seemed dark
Into my life, you brought back a spark
Of hope for a brighter tomorrow
More strength for the day
Knowing your love has helped every way
You now are the gold in my morning sun
The colors in my rainbow bright
My laughter, my comfort
My peace through the night
You now are my sunshine after the rain
You have eased my grief
Helped to erase some of the pain
You are the ingredient that in my life was missing
You bring back pleasure to hugging and kissing
We shared our sorrow, cried and prayed with each other
Have now become closer than sister or brother
I want to be near you all my life through
I thank God for his blessings of bringing me you

About the Author

Faye was born October 12, 1917, in Osbourne, Missouri.

At a very young age, her parents divorced after the traumatic death of her sister. Having to endure the loss of her sibling, the departure of her mother, she was faced with the responsibilities of helping her father raise her four brothers.

Faye married Don Parnell and together they raised five children. Their union was a true love affair of forty-six years, ending after her husband lost his long battle with cancer. She later married a close family friend, who had lost his spouse and again became a widow in 2007.

Faye discovered her love for poetry when she was a young girl of about ten. She became a Christian at that time and started writing poetry herself. Being able to express feelings of sorrow and loss and also happiness and hope through her faith provided great comfort throughout her life. Faye shared her words with family and friends and wrote of their pain and glee. Her entire life has been dedicated to her unconditional love for others and unrelenting faith of God.

The door to her heart and home are always open. Never judging, yet always encouraging others with compassion, honesty, and a loving spirit. She so desires never to miss an opportunity to spread the Word of God so others can reap the benefits of a life with the Lord.

Her collection of poetry is a gift and legacy for all.

Recently celebrating her one hundredth birthday, she attributes her longevity to her faith, love for all, healing of laughter, a healthy lifestyle, and of course, that cup of tea.

Faye resides in her home in Odessa, Missouri, remaining close to her children, ten grandchildren, and twenty-one great- and 6 great great grandchildren.

CPSIA information can be obtained
at www.ICGtesting.com
Printed in the USA
LVHW02s2331010418
571841LV00007B/55/P